FlashRevise Pocketbook

GCSE
Modern World History

Philip Allan Updates, an imprint of Hodder Education, an Hachette UK company, Market Place, Deddington, Oxfordshire OX15 0SE

Orders

Bookpoint Ltd, 130 Milton Park, Abingdon, Oxfordshire OX14 4SB
tel: 01235 827720   fax: 01235 400454   e-mail: uk.orders@bookpoint.co.uk

Lines are open 9.00 a.m.–5.00 p.m., Monday to Saturday, with a 24-hour message answering service. You can also order through our website: www.philipallan.co.uk

© Philip Allan Updates 2009
ISBN 978-1-4441-0910-8

First published in 2004 as *Flashrevise Cards*

Impression number   5   4   3   2   1
Year   2014   2013   2012   2011   2010   2009

Printed in Spain

Hachette UK's policy is to use papers that are natural, renewable and recyclable products and made from wood grown in sustainable forests. The logging and manufacturing processes are expected to conform to the environmental regulations of the country of origin.

P01633

The causes and outbreak of the First World War

1 Alliance system
2 Arms race
3 Balkan Wars, 1912–13
4 Bosnia crisis, 1908
5 Franz Ferdinand
6 Moroccan Crisis, 1905
7 Moroccan Crisis, 1911
8 Schlieffen Plan
9 Wilhelm II

The peace treaties, 1918–23

10 Clemenceau, Georges
11 Hyperinflation
12 Lloyd George, David
13 National self-determination
14 Paris Peace Conference, 1919–20
15 Reparations
16 Treaty of Brest-Litovsk, 1918
17 Treaty of Lausanne, 1923
18 Treaty of Neuilly, 1919
19 Treaty of Saint-Germain, 1919
20 Treaty of Sèvres, 1920
21 Treaty of Trianon, 1920
22 Treaty of Versailles, 1919
23 War Guilt clause
24 Wilson, Woodrow

The search for peace and stability, 1920–39

25 Abyssinian War, 1935–36
26 Collective security
27 Dawes Plan, 1924
28 Fourteen Points
29 Geneva Protocol, 1924
30 Great Depression
31 Isolationism
32 Kellogg–Briand Pact, 1928
33 League of Nations, 1920–45
34 Manchuria
35 Mussolini, Benito
36 Ruhr
37 Wall Street Crash, 1929

The collapse of international order by 1939

38 Anglo-German Naval Treaty, 1935
39 Anschluss, 1938
40 Appeasement
41 Chamberlain, Neville
42 Disarmament Conference, 1932
43 Hitler, Adolf
44 Hoare–Laval Pact, 1935
45 *Lebensraum*
46 Molotov–Ribbentrop Pact, 1939
47 Munich Agreement, 1938
48 Rhineland
49 Rome–Berlin Axis, 1936
50 Saar

Alliance system

Q1 Growing tension between several European powers at the turn of the century resulted in what?

Q2 What were the two main alliances in 1914?

Q3 Were these alliances defensive or offensive in nature?

Q4 Explain the connection between the assassination of Archduke Franz Ferdinand and the alliance system.

ANSWERS ⟩⟩

A1 the creation of two European political and military camps, each determined to be more powerful than the other

A2 the Triple Alliance (Austria-Hungary, Germany, Italy) and the Triple Entente (Britain, Russia, France)

A3 defensive: they were supposed to come into effect only if one member was attacked first

A4 the killing of Austro-Hungarian Archduke Franz Ferdinand by a Serb nationalist triggered a sequence of events centred on the alliance system, ending in the outbreak of world war

examiner's **note** The war that broke out in August had long been expected and prepared for; many people and politicians actually wanted it.

Arms race

Q1 Which two countries engaged in a naval arms race before 1914?

Q2 Explain the rivalry between them.

Q3 What was a 'dreadnought'?

Q4 The appearance of the dreadnought marked an intensifying of the arms race. Why?

ANSWERS))

continuous competition between rival countries or alliances to build stockpiles of weapons in order to secure a military advantage

A1 Britain and Germany

A2 although their royal families were related, tensions had been growing since the turn of the century; they were imperial rivals, each trying to prevent the other becoming dominant militarily

A3 a revolutionary class of British battleship built from 1906

A4 it was quicker, better armed and with thicker protective armour than any previous ship; Germany was determined to match British sea power and set about developing new ships of its own

examiner's **note** The naval arms race was a major cause of the First World War.

Balkans Wars, 1912–13

Q1 What was the outcome of these wars?

Q2 How did the outcome of the wars affect relations between Serbia and Austria?

Q3 Kaiser Wilhelm learned what important lesson from these wars?

Q4 How did Russia react to the conflicts?

ANSWERS ▶▶

series of local conflicts involving an alliance of the Balkan states against Turkey and followed by war between Serbia and Hungary

A1 Serbia was victorious in both conflicts; its size doubled, and Slavic nationalism intensified

A2 it made them even worse, as Serbs in Bosnia-Herzegovina stirred up trouble against the Austrian authorities

A3 that Austria was his only dependable ally; as a result he promised the Austrians full support in any action they took, which was to become significant following Franz Ferdinand's assassination

A4 Russia, still bitter over its climbdown during the Bosnia crisis in 1908, sought to recover some prestige in the region by declaring full support for the Serbs

***examiner's* note** These wars again showed the dangerous nature of the alliance system. The Austrians were determined to teach Serbia a lesson and looked to take full advantage of any chance to do so.

3 ANSWERS

Bosnia Crisis, 1908

Q1 The crisis was sparked by what?

Q2 List three reasons why Serbia was so outraged and ready to go to war.

Q3 A wider war seemed inevitable in 1908. How was it avoided?

Q4 In what way did this crisis contribute to the outbreak of war in 1914?

'local' conflict between Austria-Hungary and Serbia that almost resulted in European war

A1 at the turn of the century the Turkish empire was crumbling; Austria-Hungary took advantage of this by annexing the former Ottoman province of Bosnia-Herzegovina

A2 the Austro-Hungarian move put a million Serbs under Austrian control; Serbia was deprived of an outlet to the sea; Serbian dreams of a unified state (Pan-Slavism) were dashed

A3 Germany was prepared to fight and promised full support for Austria; Russia, ready to help the Serbs, backed down because its allies Britain and France did not want to get involved

A4 Serbia and Austria became bitter enemies after 1908; Serbian nationalists set up the Black Hand, an organisation committed to provoking war with Austria

examiner's **note** Russia felt humiliated by its climbdown and wanted revenge. Tsar Nicholas ordered an immediate arms build-up and strengthening of Russia's alliance with France.

 ANSWERS

Franz Ferdinand

Q1 Where and when was he assassinated?

Q2 Why was Bosnia-Herzegovina significant?

Q3 Who was responsible for his murder?

Q4 The assassination was quickly followed by what?

ANSWERS

archduke and heir to the Austro-Hungarian empire whose assassination set in motion the sequence of events that resulted in the First World War

A1 in Sarajevo, capital of Bosnia-Herzegovina, on 28 June 1914

A2 it was home to several ethnic groups, including Serbs; at the time, the Austrians governed Bosnia-Herzegovina as part of their empire

A3 Gavrilo Princip, a member of a Serb group (the Black Hand) that wanted to unite all the Serbian peoples of the Austro-Hungarian empire in an independent Serbian state

A4 an Austrian declaration of war against Serbia, backed by the Germans; Russia's alliance with Serbia, Britain and France led to the First World War.

examiner's note Some students see Franz Ferdinand's assassination as the cause of the war; it must be studied in the wider context of the alliances in order to fully understand its significance.

 ANSWERS

Moroccan Crisis, 1905

Q1 What sparked this crisis?

Q2 How did the Kaiser hope to drive Britain and France apart?

Q3 The crisis was resolved at the 1906 Algeciras Conference. Why was Germany so bitterly disappointed with the outcome?

Q4 Which important alliance came into effect in 1907?

A1 threatened by the 1904 Anglo-French Entente, Germany saw the international status of Morocco – not yet colonised but coveted by France – as an opportunity to weaken ties between London and Paris

A2 during a visit to Tangiers, Wilhelm promised the Sultan of Morocco full German support against further French expansion

A3 13 nations attended, but only Austria-Hungary supported Germany, which was forced to climb down; France secured most of its aims

A4 concerned by Germany's actions, Britain and France signed the Triple Entente with Russia; Britain and France grew stronger, not weaker

***examiner's* note** German pride was injured as the international community ignored its demands. The Kaiser saw the Triple Entente as a move by hostile powers to encircle Germany, while British suspicion of German ambitions grew deeper and tension between the two governments rose.

(6) ANSWERS

Moroccan Crisis, 1911

Q1 Why is this crisis also known as the Agadir Crisis?

Q2 How did Germany's 'flexing of muscles' backfire?

Q3 Germany was forced to accept French control of Morocco. Did Berlin gain anything?

Q4 What impact did the crisis have on relations between Britain and France?

ANSWERS

A1 it was sparked by the arrival of the German warship *Panther* at the port of Agadir in a show of force aimed at compelling France to hand over parts of the French Congo to Germany

A2 seeing the *Panther* as symbolic of the growing German naval threat, Britain mobilised the North Sea Fleet as a direct challenge to Germany, which again climbed down

A3 a small part of the Congo; more significant was Germany's loss of face

A4 brought even closer together, they promised to coordinate their foreign policies and arranged for military cooperation in the event of a German attack

examiner's **note** Bitter about the role played by Britain in supporting France, Germany increased the size of its army by funding the biggest ever peacetime increase. The French and Russian militaries responded by increasing their strength.

 7 **ANSWERS**

Schlieffen Plan

Q1 The development of this plan was influenced by which two considerations?

Q2 How did General Schlieffen, father of the plan, accommodate these?

Q3 The success or failure of the Schlieffen Plan hinged entirely on what?

Q4 List six factors that contributed to the failure of the plan.

ANSWERS

A1 France and Russia formed the Dual Alliance in 1893, which meant Germany faced possible attack on two fronts; Germany did not have the economic or material resources for a long war

A2 he believed France could be defeated in less than 6 weeks by a massive attack through Belgium; he would then turn to defeating Russia, which he believed would be slow to mobilise

A3 the speed of the German advance through Belgium and France

A4 Russian military strength; exhaustion of German forces; the speed of Russian mobilisation; strong Belgian resistance; the ability of the French to reinforce their troops; the effectiveness of the British Expeditionary Force

examiner's **note** The failure of the plan marked the end of the war of movement and the beginning of the trench warfare that is synonymous with the First World War.

Wilhelm II

Q1 What does the word *Weltpolitik* refer to?

Q2 Where did it originate?

Q3 How did *Weltpolitik* contribute to international tension?

Q4 What did Wilhelm do that intensified the arms race with Britain?

ANSWERS ▶▶

German Kaiser (emperor) (1888–1918) who led his country into the First World War

A1 Wilhelm's 'world view': he believed Germany should be a world power, with its own colonial empire

A2 it was the product of Wilhelm's strict military education, pride in sea power and envy of Britain's empire, which contributed to his desire to see Germany take its own 'place in the sun'

A3 Germany's aggressive and ambitious policy of military and economic expansion alarmed the European powers, especially Britain

A4 he ordered a build-up of the German navy; the British responded by developing a new type of battleship, the 'dreadnought'

***examiner's* note** Wilhelm's determination not just to reign but to play the leading role in German foreign policy is seen as a major cause of the international tension before 1914.

 ANSWERS

Clemenceau, Georges

Q1 What was Clemenceau's nickname? Explain its significance.

Q2 Which word best sums up Clemenceau's position during the Versailles settlement?

Q3 Was Clemenceau's attitude towards Germany shared by the other two leaders of the 'Big Three'?

Q4 Would it be accurate to say that Clemenceau was satisfied by the Treaty of Versailles?

 ANSWERS

French prime minister who was a driving force during the postwar peace settlements

A1 his gruff style earned Clemenceau the nickname 'Le Tigre', or 'Tiger'; he approached diplomacy in the same uncompromising way

A2 hatred; France had suffered greatly and Clemenceau wanted Germany severely punished and made too weak ever to invade France again

A3 no; Lloyd George was a compromiser, recognising that a harsh treaty might lead to trouble; Wilson was an idealist, wanting a more just peace

A4 no; Germany had undoubtedly been dealt with very firmly, but Clemenceau did not think this was enough and argued that Germany might still attack France

examiner's note Clemenceau's demand for harsh treatment of Germany was not forgotten by the Germans, who later responded enthusiastically to Hitler's promise to avenge Germany's humiliation.

 10 ANSWERS

Hyperinflation

Q1 What were the main causes of hyperinflation in Germany?

Q2 How did hyperinflation affect ordinary people?

Q3 Who were the biggest losers from hyperinflation?

Q4 Did Germany recover?

ANSWERS

rapid inflation, marked by rising prices
and a decline in the value of money,
which crippled Germany in 1923

A1 war reparations, the worthlessness of the mark (German currency) caused by over-circulation, and the French occupation of the Ruhr

A2 the price of goods spiralled out of control; in 1918 a loaf of bread cost 0.63 marks; in November 1923 it cost 201,000,000,000 marks

A3 small businesses were hit hard and the savings of Germany's middle class and anyone living on fixed incomes (e.g. pensioners) were wiped out

A4 yes; hyperinflation ended when the Stresemann government abolished the mark and replaced it with the Rentenmark

***examiner's* note** The losers from hyperinflation held the Weimar Republic responsible; this caused political unrest all over Germany and triggered Hitler's Beer Hall putsch.

(11) ANSWERS

Lloyd George, David

Q1 Name the leaders of France, the USA and Italy who, along with Lloyd George, made up the 'Big Four' at Paris in 1919.

Q2 State three reasons why Lloyd George wanted a compromise peace with Germany.

Q3 Lloyd George was particularly interested in the fate of Germany's colonies. Why?

Q4 Why did Lloyd George ultimately agree to Germany's harsh punishment?

ANSWERS

A1 Clemenceau, Wilson and Orlando

A2 • so the Germans would not want revenge in the future
    • so Germany would be strong enough to resist communism
    • a rebuilt German economy would be better for British trade

A3 he wanted to secure them in order to expand the British empire

A4 he had successfully campaigned in the 1918 general election on a promise to the British public to 'make Germany pay'

examiner's **note** Lloyd George complained bitterly about the Treaty of Versailles after it was signed; he believed that the reparations bill, in particular, was a recipe for future conflict.

National self-determination

Q1 Which allied war leader was most associated with the principle of self-determination after 1918?

Q2 Name the six new states established by the Paris peace treaties.

Q3 List two potential problems concerning new states in central and eastern Europe.

Q4 Was the right of self-determination extended to the peoples of the former German colonies?

ANSWERS

A1 US president Woodrow Wilson, whose Fourteen Points guided
him at the Paris Peace Conference

A2 Poland, Czechoslovakia, Yugoslavia, Finland, Estonia and Lithuania

A3 • many were small and weak and unable to defend themselves
against attack from any major power
• many had large numbers of different national groups living
within their borders

A4 no; German Samoa went to New Zealand and the former African
colonies were handed to the Allies to run as mandates

examiner's **note** Self-determination was an important factor that contributed
to the collapse of the Austro-Hungarian and Ottoman empires; the roots of the
current Arab-Israeli conflict can be traced to the latter.

(13) ANSWERS

Paris Peace Conference, 1919–20

Q1 Name the main peace treaty signed at Paris.

Q2 What three major problems faced the peacemakers as they gathered in Paris?

Q3 Some historians describe the peace conference as a 'victors' club'. Explain.

Q4 Were the treaties decided at Paris fair?

ANSWERS

A1 the Treaty of Versailles (1919) between Germany and the Allies

A2 • political chaos and economic ruin in Germany
• the differing agendas of the victorious Allies
• the desire for self-determination in central and eastern Europe

A3 the decisions were made by Britain, France and the USA; the defeated powers had no real power of negotiation

A4 historians are divided on this: some see them as unduly harsh, while others use the Treaty of Brest-Litovsk as evidence of what a victorious Germany would have done

examiner's **note** The controversial treaties drawn up at Paris contributed significantly to the breakdown of international stability in the 1930s.

Reparations

Q1 Why was the reparations clause included in the peace treaties?

Q2 What reparations figure was set for Germany at Versailles?

Q3 How realistic was it to expect Germany to pay reparations?

Q4 Did Germany ever pay the full reparations amount?

ANSWERS

compensation paid after a war by the defeated powers to the victors

A1 the First World War caused unprecedented loss of life, physical destruction and economic collapse; many blamed Germany for causing this and believed it should pay

A2 £6,600 million, payable over 42 years

A3 not very; the German economy was in ruins; the treaty deprived Germany of merchant ships, railway engines and valuable iron and coal deposits

A4 no; in 1922 the Weimar government claimed it could not continue paying; this led to tension between Germany and France; in 1931 the reparations claim was abandoned

examiner's **note** The reparations issue is closely linked to hyperinflation, the Franco-Belgian occupation of the Ruhr, and the Beer Hall putsch; they should be studied together.

Treaty of Brest-Litovsk, 1918

Q1 Why did Russia seek peace with Germany in late 1917?

Q2 Was the treaty harsh on the Russians?

Q3 Did the treaty affect Russia's relationship with its wartime allies?

Q4 This treaty is typically not included in the postwar treaties. What else do you need to know about it?

ANSWERS

peace agreement between Russia
and Germany that ended Russian
involvement in the First World War

A1 the First World War was a disaster for Russia; the Bolsheviks
    seized power in 1917 and Lenin wanted peace at any price

A2 incredibly harsh; Russia lost 74% of its iron ore and coal,
    26% of its railways, 26% of its population and 27% of its farmland;
    Germany also demanded a war indemnity of 300 million roubles

A3 yes; after the Bolsheviks withdrew from the war, Britain and
    the USA sent supplies and men to help the (anti-Bolshevik)
    White Russians in the Russian Civil War

A4 the roots of the Cold War between the Soviet Union and the
    West can be traced to the aftermath of the treaty

examiner's **note** Germany's treatment of Russia is seen as a clear indication
of how it would have dealt with a defeated France and Britain.

Treaty of Lausanne, 1923

Q1 What led the Turks to refuse the terms of the Treaty of Sèvres?

Q2 What were the main provisions of the Treaty of Lausanne?

Q3 'The immediate significance of the Treaty of Lausanne was limited to territorial gains and losses.' True or false?

Q4 Did Turkey's successful challenge to the Treaty of Sèvres lead to better or worse relations with the victorious allies?

ANSWERS ▶▶

A1 Sèvres punished Turkey harshly; in particular, the Turks resented the loss of control of Constantinople to the League of Nations

A2 Turkey got back Eastern Thrace and Smyrna, land lost to Greece at Sèvres; Constantinople and some of its old colonies were returned and demands for Turkish war reparations and disarmament were dropped

A3 false; Mustafa Kemal's challenge to Sèvres also marked the end of the old Turkish (Ottoman) empire

A4 better relations; Turkey was no longer seen as a defeated enemy but as a victor that had won its independence

***examiner's* note** Kemal's refusal to consider the Treaty of Sèvres binding, and its subsequent replacement by the Treaty of Lausanne, demonstrated that the Paris peace treaties could be challenged successfully.

(17) ANSWERS

Treaty of Neuilly, 1919

Q1 Did Bulgaria lose any territory under the treaty?

Q2 What were the other main terms?

Q3 What was the reaction in Bulgaria to the treaty?

Q4 Why were the terms imposed on Bulgaria less harsh than those for other defeated powers?

ANSWERS

A1 yes; it lost 10% of its land to Greece, Romania and Yugoslavia

A2 the Bulgarian army was limited to 20,000 men and a reparations
bill of £90 million was set

A3 a national day of mourning was declared when the details were
published; the Bulgarian leader who signed the treaty was
assassinated in 1923

A4 the victors were concerned that severe terms in the Balkans
would lead to new war in the region

examiner's **note** Bulgaria was the first of the Central Powers to surrender; this,
the Bulgarians believed, entitled them to special treatment by the victorious Allies.

(18) ANSWERS

Treaty of Saint-Germain, 1919

Q1 List four main provisions of the treaty.

Q2 What does the word 'Anschluss' mean?

Q3 Why did the Allies want Austria to be kept permanently weak?

Q4 What else was significant about the treaty?

ANSWERS

A1 • Austria lost territory to Czechoslovakia, Yugoslavia, Italy and
Romania
• its population was reduced from a pre-1914 high of 28 million
to 8 million
• the Austrian army was limited to 30,000 men
• Austria was made liable for reparations payments

A2 it refers to the union of Austria and Germany, something
forbidden in the treaty

A3 Italy feared a resurgence of Austrian power in the region

A4 it formalised the break-up of the old Austro-Hungarian Empire

***examiner's* note** The harshness of this treaty contributed to Austrian
support for Hitler after he came to power in Germany.

(19) ANSWERS

Treaty of Sèvres, 1920

Q1 What were the main provisions of the treaty?

Q2 Why was the treaty so unpopular among the Turks?

Q3 Name three middle eastern countries taken over by Britain after the break-up of the Turkish empire.

Q4 Was the treaty ever enforced?

ANSWERS ▶▶

A1 Turkey lost land to Greece, colonies in the middle east, and control of the Black Sea Straits

A2 it was signed by the unpopular ruling sultan; the Turks' refusal to accept his rule led to the revolution that put Mustafa Kemal in power, and to war with Greece

A3 Palestine, Iraq and Jordan

A4 no; Kemal's refusal to accept the terms of the treaty led to it being replaced by the Treaty of Lausanne, which contained significantly less harsh terms

***examiner's* note** The Sèvres settlement saw the beginnings of the Arab-Israeli conflict.

Treaty of Trianon, 1920

Q1 Why was there a delay in the signing of this treaty?

Q2 Was the treaty harsh on Hungary?

Q3 Did the treaty address fully the issue of self-determination in the region?

Q4 How did the treaty seek to prevent a resurgent Hungary?

ANSWERS

A1 it was not signed until a communist uprising was suppressed by a right-wing dictatorship

A2 yes; it lost two-thirds of its territory and inhabitants, it was made liable for reparations and the Hungarian army was limited to 35,000 men

A3 no; it left sizeable minorities in neighbouring countries

A4 it paralysed the Hungarian economy and infrastructure; new borders were drawn up to cut off important road and rail lines from Hungarian territory

examiner's note Hungarian foreign policy between the wars was dominated by attempts to get the treaty revised or changed.

Treaty of Versailles, 1919

Q1 What were four main clauses of the treaty?

Q2 Which two provisions did the Germans object to most strongly?

Q3 The word 'Diktat' refers to what?

Q4 Was the treaty fair?

ANSWERS

A1
- Germany lost land in Europe and its overseas empire to the Allies
- it was allowed a 100,000-man army
- it was not allowed to join the League of Nations
- Anschluss (union) with Austria was forbidden

A2 reparations of £6,600 million; Article 231, which totally blamed
Germany for starting the war

A3 a strong feeling among the German people that the treaty was a
dictated peace in which Germany was given no right of negotiation
whatsoever

A4 some historians argue it was unfair because it reflected Allied
desire for revenge; others argue it could have been much worse
for Germany

examiner's **note** Learn this treaty. It appears frequently in questions about
how German resentment towards it helped Hitler come to power.

War Guilt clause

Q1 By what other name is the War Guilt clause known?

Q2 Why was it important for the Allies to blame Germany for the war?

Q3 Did the Germans have any opportunity to veto the War Guilt clause?

Q4 Of all the provisions of the treaty, the War Guilt clause was the most resented by the Germans. Why?

ANSWERS ▶▶

A1 Article 231

A2 by making Germany accept total blame, the Allies were able to justify their demands for reparations

A3 no; they were told that if they did not sign the treaty, Germany would be invaded and occupied by the Allies

A4 not only did it make Germany liable for reparations, but it also reinforced the utter shame, anger and helplessness felt by the German people

***examiner's* note** A good understanding of the impact of the clause is essential for explaining German opposition to the treaty and Hitler's rise to power.

(23) ANSWERS

Wilson, Woodrow

Q1 List Wilson's main goals at Paris.

Q2 What did Wilson believe to be the key to future peace?

Q3 Name the organisation that Wilson wanted formed to prevent further wars.

Q4 Wilson failed to achieve most of his immediate goals. Give two reasons why.

ANSWERS

A1 lasting peace; self-determination for the different nationalities; to avoid US troops having to fight on European soil again

A2 his Fourteen Points

A3 the League of Nations

A4 • he did not understand the deep enmity between France and Germany
  • he was pressured by the French and Lloyd George to punish Germany severely and had to compromise

examiner's **note** The US Senate refused to ratify the Treaty of Versailles; while travelling around the USA in 1920 to win support for his ideas, Wilson suffered a stroke.

Abyssinian War, 1935–36

Q1 Why did Mussolini invade Abyssinia?

Q2 Name the Abyssinian leader who appealed to the League of Nations for help.

Q3 What was the response of the international community to Italian aggression?

Q4 Was there anything the League could have done to discourage Mussolini?

ANSWERS

A1 to create an empire modelled on ancient Rome; to increase his
    popularity; to avenge an earlier defeat in 1896

A2 Haile Selassie

A3 the League of Nations condemned Italy but did nothing to
    prevent the Italian conquest

A4 yes; it could have closed the Suez Canal or banned oil sales to
    Italy

examiner's **note** The lack of a coherent international response to the Italian
invasion revealed the flawed notion of collective security.

Collective security

Q1 In which document was the idea of collective security set out?

Q2 What three steps was the League of Nations to take to deal with aggression?

Q3 What did the League require from members to make collective security work?

Q4 Why did the US refusal to join the League seriously undermine collective security?

ANSWERS

A1 the Covenant (rules, aims and procedures) of the League of Nations

A2 • condemn the aggressor and tell it to stop
    • impose economic sanctions
    • use military force

A3 goodwill; political backing; material support

A4 it was the only country powerful enough to guarantee
    international support for the League

***examiner's* note** The unwillingness of member states to follow through was
a major factor in the failure of the League as a peacekeeping organisation.

Dawes Plan, 1924

Q1 What did the Dawes Plan attempt to tackle?

Q2 What three measures did the plan call for?

Q3 Was the plan a success?

Q4 In what two ways was the plan a turning point?

ANSWERS ▸▸

A1 hyperinflation and the collapse of the German economy in 1923

A2 • reduction in reparations
• reorganisation of the German currency
• international loans to Germany

A3 in a limited way; it gave Germany superficial and temporary relief from its debt problem

A4 • it marked the beginning of changing attitudes towards Germany
• it opened the way for German economic recovery

***examiner's* note** US money that poured into Germany went around in circles — Germany used it to pay reparations to France and Britain; they used it to pay off war loans to the USA.

Fourteen Points

Q1 The Fourteen Points reflected Wilson's two main goals. What were they?

Q2 Why did the British government object to the second of the Fourteen Points, which called for freedom of the seas in peace and war?

Q3 Did the leaders of the other victorious powers support the Fourteen Points?

Q4 What lasting impact did the Fourteen Points have?

ANSWERS

US president Woodrow Wilson's
plan for securing international
peace and stability after 1918

A1 • to prevent another war
• to achieve national self-determination

A2 British global influence rested on sea power and Lloyd George
did not want this advantage neutralised

A3 ultimately, no; Lloyd George was, at first, supportive but the British
wanted to 'make Germany pay'; Clemenceau wanted revenge; the
Italian leader, Orlando, was more interested in territorial gains

A4 little; the League of Nations was established to resolve conflict,
but it never worked as Wilson hoped

***examiner's* note** The Fourteen Points failed to create the new world order
that Wilson envisaged. Lloyd George and Clemenceau were motivated by
revenge rather than Wilson's idealism.

Geneva Protocol, 1924

Q1 Who was the driving force behind the Geneva Protocol?

Q2 How was the protocol intended to strengthen the Covenant of the League of Nations?

Q3 Which body did the protocol authorise to settle disputes through arbitration?

Q4 Give two reasons why the protocol came to nothing.

ANSWERS

A1 British prime minister Ramsay MacDonald

A2 it defined an aggressor nation as any country that refused to accept arbitration

A3 the Permanent Court of International Justice

A4 • Ramsay MacDonald lost power the same year
    • the new British government did not want to be compelled to accept the League's decisions

examiner's **note** The failure of this initiative demonstrated how national self-interest took priority over international cooperation.

Great Depression

Q1 Which event is most associated with the Great Depression?

Q2 What impact did the Depression have on Europe?

Q3 Did the Depression affect international relations?

Q4 How was economic recovery achieved?

ANSWERS

A1 the Wall Street Crash in October 1929

A2 millions of Europeans lost their jobs

A3 yes; the decline in world trade damaged relations and led to increased threats to peace and stability

A4 employment increased as war became more likely and governments geared their economies to arms production

examiner's **note** Relations between countries soured as the Depression continued to 'bite' and this contributed to the outbreak of the Second World War.

Isolationism

Q1 Which country is most associated with isolation during the early twentieth century?

Q2 Why was isolationism popular with most Americans?

Q3 How was Europe affected by post-1918 American isolationism?

Q4 What does the term 'economic isolationism' mean and why is it significant?

ANSWERS

a policy of non-participation in alliances with other countries or in their affairs

A1 the USA; isolationism was the recurring theme of its foreign policy

A2 some 100,000 US soldiers died in the First World War; the USA also feared the spread of European revolutionary ideas like communism

A3 Congress rejected the peace treaties and refused to join the League of Nations; this isolationist attitude prevented the USA from playing the crucial role in ensuring European peace and stability

A4 the US government set high taxes on all imported foreign goods; this led to retaliation by other countries and contributed to the Great Depression of the 1930s

***examiner's* note** US isolationism is an important topic; the absence of US power and influence throughout the interwar period became a crucial factor as international peace and stability collapsed.

Kellogg–Briand Pact, 1928

Q1 By what other name is this pact known?

Q2 What were the two main objectives of the pact?

Q3 Why did it prove ineffective?

Q4 Was the Kellogg–Briand Pact a complete failure?

ANSWERS ❯❯

A1 the Pact of Paris

A2 65 countries agreed to renounce war as an instrument of foreign policy and to resolve all conflicts by peaceful means

A3 it lacked real authority and did not provide any way to enforce its terms; these could be carried out only if countries kept their word

A4 no; it helped to involve the USA again in international affairs

examiner's **note** The pact was seen as a significant step towards the peaceful resolution of international conflict; in reality it demonstrated the failure of collective security.

League of Nations, 1920–45

Q1 Which leader proposed the establishment of a League of Nations?

Q2 Name three important countries whose non-membership between 1919 and 1935 significantly weakened its effectiveness.

Q3 List four reasons why the League proved ultimately ineffective.

Q4 Was the League able to achieve anything?

ANSWERS

A1 US president Woodrow Wilson called for it as one of his Fourteen Points

A2 the USA, Germany and the USSR

A3 • no armed force to impose sanctions
• slow to make decisions
• seen as a 'victors' club'
• undermined by member states following their own agendas

A4 yes; in the 1920s it helped return refugees, reduced diseases, stopped slave labour and settled disputes between smaller member states

examiner's **note** Questions on the League of Nations often focus on the issue of whether or not it was doomed to fail from the start.

Manchuria

Q1 Give two reasons for Japanese interest in Manchuria.

Q2 What incident did the Japanese use as an excuse to invade?

Q3 What name did the Japanese give to the conquered territory?

Q4 How did the League of Nations react to the Japanese invasion?

ANSWERS

A1 • it would provide a market for Japanese goods
   • it could supply Japan with important raw materials (coal and iron ore)

A2 they faked an incident between Chinese and Japanese soldiers at Mukden

A3 it was renamed Manchukuo

A4 it sent the Lytton Commission to investigate; Japan responded to international condemnation by leaving the League in 1933

***examiner's* note** The invasion revealed the powerlessness of the League of Nations in the face of determined aggression.

Mussolini, Benito

Q1 When did Mussolini found the Fascist Party?

Q2 What term was used to describe his fascist dictatorship?

Q3 Did he achieve much for his country?

Q4 What were the circumstances of his fall from power?

ANSWERS

A1 in 1919 as an anti-democratic and anti-socialist organisation

A2 corporate state

A3 no; his domestic successes were few and his expansionist foreign
policy led to an alliance with Hitler and disaster in the Second
World War

A4 he was forced to resign in 1943, and executed by Italian
communists in 1945

examiner's note Mussolini's rise to power served as a model for politically
ambitious strongmen and was the inspiration for Hitler's Beer Hall putsch.

(35) ANSWERS

Ruhr

Q1 Why did the French and Belgians march into the Ruhr?

Q2 How did the Ruhr Germans respond to the occupation?

Q3 List three consequences of the occupation for the German people.

Q4 What was the outcome of the occupation?

ANSWERS

A1 the German economy was in ruins, and it could not afford to pay reparations; the French and Belgians wanted control of the Ruhr

A2 with a campaign of 'passive resistance' — strikes and non-cooperation

A3 • rising unemployment
• fewer goods in the shops and skyrocketing prices
• hyperinflation

A4 the occupying forces left after Weimar leader Gustav Stresemann resumed reparations payments using the new Rentenmark currency

examiner's **note** The occupation was condemned by the British and US governments, brought little real benefit to the French, further undermined the Weimar Republic and contributed to the Beer Hall putsch.

Wall Street Crash, 1929

Q1 What triggered this event?

Q2 List four consequences of the Wall Street Crash.

Q3 How did people paying for goods in instalments contribute to the disastrous aftermath of the crash?

Q4 Did the crash impact on Europe?

ANSWERS

A1 a panic on the stock market; millions of shares changed hands and the market collapsed

A2 • shareholders were ruined
• many banks went broke
• personal savings were wiped out
• unemployment skyrocketed

A3 people who became unemployed could not keep up their repayments, so their goods were repossessed

A4 yes; US companies reacted by withdrawing their overseas investments and international relations worsened

***examiner's* note** While the Wall Street Crash was an important feature of the interwar economic crisis, it did not in itself cause the Depression.

Anglo-German Naval Treaty, 1935

Q1 This treaty caused the collapse of which agreement between Britain, France and Italy?

Q2 How were British-French relations affected by the Anglo-German Naval Treaty?

Q3 Why did Britain agree to this treaty?

Q4 Name three ways in which Hitler gained from the treaty.

ANSWERS

A1 the Stresa Front

A2 they were damaged; the French were upset because Britain signed the treaty unilaterally and without first consulting them

A3 it saw agreement with Hitler as a way to guarantee its continuing naval superiority

A4 • it brought the Nazi regime out of diplomatic isolation
    • it allowed German rearmament
    • it undermined attempts to build a united front against Germany

examiner's **note** By signing this treaty, the British government helped Hitler break the Treaty of Versailles.

Anschluss, 1938

Q1 Which treaty banned the union of Austria and Germany?

Q2 Who was Kurt Schuschnigg?

Q3 Why did Austrian support for closer ties with Germany increase in the 1930s?

Q4 What did the absence of international opposition to the Anschluss encourage Hitler to do?

ANSWERS

the forced annexation (takeover) of Austria by Germany

A1 the Treaty of Versailles

A2 he succeeded Dolfuss as Austrian leader after Dolfuss was murdered by Austrian Nazis

A3 the Austrian economy was continuing to suffer the effects of the Great Depression, while Germany was prospering

A4 to set his sights next on Czechoslovakia

***examiner's* note** Britain and France did nothing to prevent Anschluss; at the time many felt the Treaty of Versailles was in need of revision. Furthermore, Italy was allied to Germany by the Rome–Berlin Axis.

Appeasement

Q1 Which two countries had appeasement as the cornerstone of their foreign policy towards Germany and Italy in the late 1930s?

Q2 Which political leader is typically seen as the embodiment of appeasement?

Q3 State four major reasons for the policy of appeasement.

Q4 Why was 1938 a decisive turning point for the policy of appeasement?

ANSWERS ▶▶

policy of giving in to the demands of an
aggressor in the hope of avoiding conflict

A1 Britain and France

A2 British prime minister Neville Chamberlain

A3 • Britain was not ready for war
    • fear of communism among the western European powers
    • memories of the horrors of the First World War
    • Chamberlain trusted Hitler's word

A4 without first consulting the Czechs, Chamberlain and the French
    leader Daladier handed Hitler the Sudetenland

***examiner's* note** British appeasement of Hitler actually began before
Chamberlain, and it remained popular with the majority of the British people
right up to 1939.

Chamberlain, Neville

Q1 Chamberlain is closely associated with which controversial foreign policy?

Q2 Give four reasons why Chamberlain followed a policy of appeasement.

Q3 When and why did Chamberlain abandon appeasement?

Q4 Was appeasement Chamberlain's greatest foreign policy failure?

ANSWERS

Conservative prime minister of Britain, 1937–40

A1 the appeasement of the European dictators during the late 1930s

A2 • he hated war
   • Britain needed time to rearm for war
   • he believed Hitler's promises
   • there was little public support for another war with Germany

A3 in March 1939, the German invasion of Czechoslovakia convinced Chamberlain that only war would stop Hitler

A4 no; he failed to secure an alliance with the USSR — this was a real possibility and would, in effect, have surrounded Germany by allies

***examiner's* note** Chamberlain's long career of public service is defined by appeasement and historians have traditionally been harsh on him. However, any debate on the causes of the Second World War should not focus solely on appeasement.

Disarmament Conference, 1932

Q1 Name the three major powers present at this conference.

Q2 Was this the first attempt by the Europeans to secure peace through disarmament?

Q3 Germany was the driving force behind calls for this conference. Explain why.

Q4 Did the 1932 conference achieve anything?

ANSWERS

gathering of European countries to
discuss foreign and military policies
1935

A1 Britain, France and Germany

A2 no; a world disarmament conference met in 1926 but failed to
agree on a definition of 'armaments' or how they were to be
counted

A3 in 1930, now a member of the League of Nations, Germany called
for a revision of the terms of the Treaty of Versailles

A4 no; when Hitler came to power in 1933 he immediately withdrew
Germany from the conference and it broke up formally in 1934

examiner's note The failure of this conference is seen by many historians as
the first step towards the Second World War.

Hitler, Adolf

Q1 What was the Beer Hall putsch?

Q2 Name the book, written by Hitler in 1924, in which he set out his main political philosophy and aims.

Q3 Who did Hitler blame for Germany's post-1918 problems?

Q4 Hitler had three main foreign policy objectives. What were they?

ANSWERS

A1 Hitler's first attempt to seize power in Germany, in 1923

A2 *Mein Kampf* (*My Struggle*)

A3 the so-called 'November criminals' and international Jewry

A4 • to destroy the provisions of the Treaty of Versailles
  • to unite all German-speaking people in one country
  • *Lebensraum* — to expand German land in the east (ultimately into the USSR)

***examiner's* note** Hitler was responsible for Germany's military defeat in the Second World War and for the deaths of millions of people both inside and outside Germany.

Hoare–Laval Pact, 1935

Q1 To what did Britain and France agree?

Q2 Give two reasons why Britain and France were prepared to sign away Abyssinian sovereignty.

Q3 The agreement met strong resistance in Britain. Why?

Q4 Did the three European countries follow through with the pact?

ANSWERS ▶▶

agreement between the British and
French foreign ministers over Abyssinia
following the Italian invasion

193
195

A1 Italy was to be allowed to keep two-thirds of Abyssinia, including the coast

A2 • they were looking for Italian support against a resurgent Germany
• they wanted Mussolini to stop his invasion

A3 it was seen for what it was: a clear and early example of appeasement

A4 no; public outcry led to Hoare's resignation, the plan was dropped and Mussolini completed his conquest of Abyssinia

examiner's note This pact weakened the League of Nations (Italy withdrew in 1937); Anglo-French criticism of Mussolini weakened the Stresa Front and Italy was drawn closer to Hitler.

Lebensraum

Q1 Why did Hitler believe that the German people needed more living space?

Q2 State the other two key aims of Hitler's foreign policy.

Q3 Which country did Hitler believe Germany ultimately needed to conquer in order to have sufficient living space?

Q4 In what way is *Lebensraum* linked to Hitler's racial policies?

ANSWERS

'living space' — the slogan of German expansionism that was a major aim of Hitler's foreign policy

A1 he argued that Germany was overcrowded and did not have enough food and raw materials

A2 • to unite all German-speaking people in one country
• to destroy the provisions of the Treaty of Versailles

A3 the USSR; this and his hatred of communism led to the German invasion in 1941

A4 he believed that the land Germany needed was populated by what he called 'minor nations' and 'inferior races'

examiner's note *Lebensraum* made war between Germany and the USSR inevitable.

Molotov–Ribbentrop Pact, 1939

Q1 By what other names is this agreement often known?

Q2 What were the two main provisions of the pact?

Q3 The pact included several secret clauses. What did these provide for?

Q4 How did the Nazi and Soviet leaders each benefit from the pact?

ANSWERS

A1 the Nazi-Soviet Pact and the Hitler–Stalin Pact

A2 • the two countries agreed not to go to war with each other for 10 years
    • both sides pledged neutrality in the event that either became involved in a war

A3 the carving up of Poland, Finland, Lithuania and Latvia

A4 Hitler avoided the threat of war on two fronts (east and west), while Stalin gained time and space as barriers against Germany

***examiner's* note** This was a temporary 'marriage of convenience' between two dictators. It made war over Poland inevitable and ended any possibility of an east–west alliance to surround Nazi Germany.

Munich Agreement, 1938

Q1 Which countries were represented at Munich?

Q2 The leaders of these countries gathered to decide the fate of which strip of land?

Q3 Which countries, other than Germany, also acquired land at the expense of the Czechs?

Q4 Why is March 1939 a significant month in relation to the Munich Agreement?

ANSWERS

A1 Germany, Italy, Britain, France; the Czechs were not invited

A2 the Sudetenland of Czechoslovakia; this event marked the height
of British and French appeasement of Hitler

A3 Poland and Hungary

A4 in violation of the Munich Agreement, German troops took over
the remainder of Czechoslovakia; Britain and France abandoned
appeasement and prepared for war

examiner's **note** Historians are divided over the Munich Agreement.
Its defenders argue that it gave the West a vital year to improve military
preparedness; critics reply that the British and French failed to seize a real
opportunity to unite with the Czechs to make a powerful military alliance
against Hitler.

 **47** **ANSWERS**

Rhineland

Q1 What did the Treaty of Versailles decide about the future of the Rhineland?

Q2 Why did Hitler's generals oppose his plan to remilitarise the Rhineland?

Q3 How did the British and French react to this violation of the Treaty of Versailles?

Q4 Give three main consequences of the remilitarisation.

ANSWERS

A1 it demilitarised German territory west of the Rhine River and on a 50 km strip east of the river

A2 they feared that much stronger French forces would successfully resist their plans

A3 they did nothing; their willingness to stand aside was part of a wider policy of appeasement

A4 • Britain and France began to rearm
  • France had German troops on its border
  • collective security was further undermined

***examiner's* note** Remilitarisation greatly increased Hitler's popularity in Germany and boosted his confidence in foreign policy matters; within 2 years he had secured the Anschluss and the annexation of the Sudetenland.

Rome–Berlin Axis, 1936

Q1 What two events drew Mussolini closer to Hitler?

Q2 Which pre-Second World War conflict in Europe saw the two countries fighting together?

Q3 The agreement was followed by two more important political pacts involving the two countries. Name them.

Q4 What did the Rome–Berlin Axis clear the way for Hitler to do?

ANSWERS

A1 • the Italian invasion of Abyssinia
   • the League of Nations' subsequent decision to impose sanctions
     on Italy

A2 the Spanish Civil War

A3 • the Anti-Comintern Pact (1937)
   • the Pact of Steel (1939)

A4 occupy Austria and complete the Anschluss

***examiner's* note** The Axis marked a significant reversal of Italian foreign
policy, particularly as it was signed a year after Mussolini agreed to the Stresa
Front with Britain and France.

Saar

Q1 Why was the Saar so important?

Q2 What did the Treaty of Versailles decide about the Saar?

Q3 What three options did voters have in 1935? What did they decide?

Q4 Was Hitler pleased by the vote?

ANSWERS

A1 it contained large coalfields, iron ore and steel factories

A2 the League of Nations was to control it for 15 years and then a plebiscite (vote) was to decide its future

A3 • to remain under League control
• to return to Germany
• to become part of France
over 90% voted to return to Germany

A4 very much so; not only did he gain important resources, but the vote was the first step towards the union of all Germans in Germany

examiner's **note** The overwhelming vote in favour of a return to Germany was seen by Hitler as an indication of popular support for his government and policies.

50 **ANSWERS**

Sino-Japanese War, 1937–45

Q1 Which incident in 1937 sparked full-scale hostilities?

Q2 What earlier event set the stage for war between the two countries?

Q3 Did China approach the international community for assistance?

Q4 What was the Greater East Asia Co-Prosperity Sphere?

ANSWERS

A1 a clash between Chinese and Japanese troops at Marco Polo Bridge, near Beijing

A2 the Japanese invasion and subsequent occupation of Manchuria in 1931

A3 yes; it appealed to the League of Nations, but the idea of collective security had died in the mid-1930s

A4 the propaganda name given by Japan to the territories it conquered, including Manchuria and parts of China

examiner's **note** The failure of the international community to react decisively to the Japanese invasion of China led the Japanese to act even more aggressively in the years to come.

Spanish Civil War, 1936–39

Q1 Who was Francisco Franco?

Q2 Which groups backed the Republican government?

Q3 Name the Spanish town that was destroyed by German bombers in a foreshadowing of what was to come during the Second World War.

Q4 What was the significance of the Spanish Civil War?

ANSWERS

A1 leader of the Nationalist forces, which included the Catholic church, landowners and a small Fascist party

A2 Socialists, liberals, Communists and other left-wingers

A3 Guernica

A4 it divided Europe along ideological grounds and made the idea of another European war acceptable again

examiner's **note** Several foreign governments took part to help the side whose ideas they supported. Mussolini and Hitler supported Franco, while the USSR backed the Republican side. Britain and France remained neutral — a decision that contributed to the Nationalist victory.

Stresa Front, 1935

Q1 Name the three events closely tied to German foreign policy that led to the Stresa Front.

Q2 What was the outcome of the meeting of the leaders at Stresa?

Q3 Two events caused the front to collapse quickly. What were they?

Q4 Which treaty between Hitler and Mussolini demonstrated the failure of the Stresa Front?

 ANSWERS

attempt by the leaders of France, Britain and Italy to block growing German militarisation

A1 • the attempted coup by Austrian Nazis
   • the Saar plebiscite
   • the open reintroduction of conscription by Hitler

A2 the three countries condemned the reintroduction of conscription and agreed to stand together against German aggression

A3 • Britain upset France by signing the Anglo-German Naval Treaty (1935)
   • Italy invaded Abyssinia (1936)

A4 the Rome–Berlin Axis (October 1936)

***examiner's* note** The Stresa Front provided an early and real opportunity to block the aggressive expansionism of Hitler. The reasons behind its short life help to explain how and why future attempts to do the same proved unsuccessful.

Sudetenland

Q1 Which post-1918 peace treaty created the state of Czechoslovakia?

Q2 Why was occupation of the Sudetenland an early priority for Hitler?

Q3 Which agreement transferred the Sudetenland to German control?

Q4 Was Hitler satisfied with control of the Sudetenland?

ANSWERS

A1 the Treaty of Saint-Germain (1920)

A2 it was inhabited by some 3 million German-speaking people and contained rich natural resources

A3 the Munich Agreement (1938)

A4 no; he violated the agreement when he ordered the invasion of Czechoslovakia proper in March 1939, thereby starting the countdown to the Second World War

examiner's note A good understanding of the fate of the Sudetenland is essential to explaining appeasement.

Berlin airlift, 1948–49

Q1 Why did the Allies fall out over the future of Germany?

Q2 What led the Soviets to cut off West Berlin?

Q3 How did the Western powers break the blockade?

Q4 Did the Soviets try to prevent this?

ANSWERS

A1 Stalin wanted Germany to remain weak while the Western powers wanted to see it prosper

A2 disagreement between East and West over a new German currency resulted in a Soviet blockade of all road and rail links

A3 by flying thousands of tonnes of supplies into West Berlin

A4 no; Stalin did not want to risk war at a time when the West had the atomic bomb and the Soviets did not, so he called off the blockade

examiner's **note** The episode caused a serious deterioration of relations and led to the long-term separation of East and West Germany.

Cold War

Q1 What was the origin of the term 'Cold War'?

Q2 Can the roots of mistrust between East and West be found any earlier than 1945?

Q3 Which two meetings between the Allied leaders signalled the start of the Cold War?

Q4 List four ways in which the USA and USSR used other countries to undermine their opponent.

ANSWERS ▶▶

A1 it was first used by an American in 1947 to describe hostilities between the two sides which avoided direct conflict, or 'hot war'

A2 yes; the origins of the Cold War can be found in 1917 and the Communist victory in Russia

A3 Yalta (February 1945) and Potsdam (May 1945)

A4 • both fought each other's allies
    • both helped their respective allies fight each other
    • both supported different sides in civil wars
    • both used force to get rid of governments or movements sympathetic to the other side

***examiner's* note** The latter half of the twentieth century was dominated by the Cold War. Virtually every international conflict fought at this time can be linked to it.

Iron Curtain

Q1 Which leader first used the phrase 'Iron Curtain'?

Q2 How did the Soviet Union react to his powerful speech?

Q3 What, exactly, was the 'Iron Curtain'?

Q4 Name seven countries that found themselves on the Soviet side of the curtain.

ANSWERS

A1 British prime minister Winston Churchill in a speech at Fulton, Missouri, in 1946

A2 it called his comments a declaration of war by the West against eastern Europe

A3 a 2,000-kilometre stretch of barbed wire, sentry posts and blocked roads that dominated the political geography of post-1945 Europe

A4 East Germany, Poland, Czechoslovakia, Hungary, Romania, Bulgaria and Albania

examiner's **note** Churchill's remarks fed a growing belief among US officials that only a tough approach would work with the USSR, and led to a deterioration of East–West relations.

Korean War, 1950–53

Q1 Name the respective leaders of North and South Korea.

Q2 Why did North Korean forces invade South Korea on 25 June 1950?

Q3 Why did the USA send troops to fight in the conflict?

Q4 How did the Korean War end?

ANSWERS ▶▶

A1 Kim Il Sung; Syngman Rhee

A2 the country was divided along the 38th parallel; the Communist government in the north wanted authority over the whole country

A3 it considered the North Korean invasion a clear case of Soviet aggression

A4 the armistice signed in 1953 left Korea divided along the 38th parallel into two separate countries

examiner's **note** The war resulted in the entrenchment of military containment as US policy.

Marshall Aid

Q1 From where did Marshall Aid get its name?

Q2 What did Marshall Aid involve?

Q3 Was this support available only to the USA's allies?

Q4 Marshall Aid was a key component of which US foreign policy?

ANSWERS

A1 from US secretary of state George Marshall, who believed post-1945 European poverty was a breeding ground for communism

A2 between 1947 and 1952 the USA provided 16 European countries with $13 billion worth of food, fuel and vehicles

A3 no; the offer of aid was open to all countries but Stalin refused to allow the east Europeans to take part

A4 the Truman Doctrine; this stated that communism could not be allowed to spread in Europe

examiner's **note** Marshall Aid was a key component of containment, which strengthened western Europe against the threat of communism.

59 ANSWERS

Potsdam Conference, 1945

Q1 Name the three leaders present at Potsdam.

Q2 On what points did they agree at Potsdam?

Q3 On what issues did they disagree?

Q4 What new development in the war against Japan increased the tension at Potsdam?

ANSWERS

A1 Attlee, who replaced Churchill as the British representative, Stalin, who represented the USSR, and Truman, who represented the USA

A2 Germany to be split into four zones; Germany to be disarmed; Nazi Party to be abolished; war criminals to be prosecuted; Germany to pay reparations

A3 the future of Poland; the amount of reparations to be paid by Germany; democratic elections in eastern Europe

A4 the USA test-exploded the first atomic bomb the day before the conference started

examiner's note The new Western leaders strongly disliked Stalin and left the meeting convinced that all the USSR would understand was force. This and Truman's refusal to share atomic secrets with Stalin led to the onset of the Cold War.

Stalin, Joseph

Q1 Name the agreement made by Stalin with Nazi Germany in August 1939.

Q2 Stalin met twice with the leaders of the USA and Britain in 1945 to discuss the postwar settlement. Where did these meetings take place?

Q3 What was Stalin's main aim for Eastern Europe after 1945?

Q4 Which crisis almost resulted in war between Stalin and the Western powers?

ANSWERS

A1 the Nazi–Soviet Non-Aggression Pact

A2 Yalta and Potsdam

A3 to make sure governments were loyal to the USSR

A4 the Berlin blockade and airlift

***examiner's* note** Stalin was one of the most significant world leaders of the twentieth century. He and Adolf Hitler remain the most powerful dictators the world has seen.

Truman Doctrine, 1947

Q1 During which European conflict was this doctrine first put to the test?

Q2 Which American foreign policy was closely connected to the Truman Doctrine?

Q3 Name the American plan to inject economic aid into Europe.

Q4 How did Stalin respond to the Truman Doctrine?

ANSWERS

A1 the Greek Civil War in 1947, when US money and military advisers helped the Greek government defeat Communist rebels

A2 containment

A3 Marshall Aid

A4 he criticised it as part of a US plan for world domination, and set up Cominform to counter it

examiner's **note** The Truman Doctrine divided Europe into the Communist-controlled East and capitalist West.

Warsaw Pact, 1955

Q1 The Warsaw Pact was set up following what event?

Q2 Name the eight original member states.

Q3 What were member states pledged to do?

Q4 How did the USSR view the Warsaw Pact?

ANSWERS

A1 West Germany's entry into NATO

A2 Albania, Bulgaria, Czechoslovakia, East Germany, Hungary, Poland, Romania and the USSR

A3 to establish an agreement on mutual defence against any threatened attack; to respect each other's independence and sovereignty

A4 as a means to control its neighbours; in 1968, Warsaw Pact troops invaded Czechoslovakia

***examiner's* note** The Warsaw Pact and the North Atlantic Treaty Organization divided Europe into two massive armed camps for over 35 years. In that time, each remained on constant alert.

Yalta Conference, 1945

Q1 Name the three leaders present at Yalta.

Q2 The leaders agreed on three main issues. What were they?

Q3 Name the international peace-keeping organisation called for at Yalta.

Q4 Why was the future of Poland a 'sticking point'?

ANSWERS

wartime meeting to discuss policy towards Europe following victory in the Second World War

A1
- Churchill (UK)
- Stalin (USSR)
- Roosevelt (USA)

A2
- the Soviet pledge to invade Japanese-held Manchuria
- Germany (and Berlin) to be divided into four zones of occupation
- democratic elections to be held in all countries freed from Nazi rule

A3 the United Nations Organisation

A4 Stalin was determined to retain Soviet-occupied eastern Poland as a buffer zone; the outcome favoured the USSR

***examiner's* note** This conference was the high point in the wartime alliance, as each leader left with something he wanted. But suspicion grew and by the time of the Potsdam meeting 5 months later conditions had been created for future Cold War.

Bay of Pigs, 1961

Q1 Name the Cuban leader at the time of the invasion.

Q2 What did the US government hope a small landing on Cuba would lead to?

Q3 How successful were the landings at the Bay of Pigs?

Q4 The failure of the invasion led directly to which international crisis a year later?

ANSWERS

A1 Fidel Castro

A2 a popular uprising against Castro's rule; this proved a disastrous
miscalculation

A3 the invasion was a dismal failure; Cuban forces quickly routed the
poorly trained and badly equipped attackers

A4 the Cuban Missile Crisis

examiner's note The invasion led to a rapid deterioration of US-Cuban
relations. Castro's popularity with his people increased and he moved Cuba
strongly towards Khrushchev for protection.

Brinkmanship

Q1 Which US secretary of state from 1952 to 1959 is closely associated with this policy?

Q2 US foreign policy during this time sought to pressurise Communist states using three main measures. What were they?

Q3 Which event of 1956 represents a failure of this policy?

Q4 What was the most famous (and dangerous) example of brinkmanship?

ANSWERS

A1 John Foster Dulles

A2 • alliances between non-Communist countries
    • more sophisticated and expensive weapons
    • spreading anti-Communist and pro-West propaganda

A3 the Soviet invasion of Hungary — the USA offered no support
    and stood by as the Hungarians were crushed

A4 President Kennedy's stance during the Cuban Missile Crisis

examiner's **note** The right-wing attitude of Dulles often allowed the USSR
to appear as the 'champion' of states opposed to US 'colonialism'.

Castro, Fidel

Q1 Name the right-wing Cuban dictator overthrown by Castro and his supporters.

Q2 Why was the USA opposed to Castro's rule?

Q3 Which event marked the first (failed) attempt by the US government to oust Castro from power?

Q4 What did Castro's friendship with Soviet leader Khrushchev encourage Moscow to do?

ANSWERS ▶▶

A1 Fulgencio Batista

A2 when he came to power Castro confiscated US-owned land and oil companies, and set up a Marxist regime

A3 the Bay of Pigs invasion (1961)

A4 to send nuclear missiles and military personnel to Cuba; this led to the Cuban Missile Crisis in 1962

***examiner's* note** Castro was one of the last remaining revolutionaries and leader of one of the few communist states still existing.

Containment

Q1 What were the two main components of the policy of containment?

Q2 How did President Truman intend to 'contain' the spread of communism?

Q3 During which European conflict was containment first implemented?

Q4 In which two conflicts did the USA become involved as part of its policy of containment in the late 1940s and early 1950s?

ANSWERS

A1 • the Truman Doctrine
   • Marshall Aid

A2 by supplying money, weapons and advisers to friendly states to help them prevent expansion of the USSR

A3 the Greek Civil War; the USA provided the Royalist side with $400 million in aid

A4 • the Berlin airlift (1948–49)
   • the Korean War (1950–53)

***examiner's* note** The introduction of containment in 1947 marked the permanent end of the USA's isolationism and demonstrated its preparedness to play a leading role in international relations.

Cuban Missile Crisis, 1962

Q1 Why did the USSR put nuclear missile bases on Cuba?

Q2 Why was the USA determined to see the removal of Soviet missiles from Cuba?

Q3 What did President Kennedy agree to in return for the removal of Soviet missiles from Cuba?

Q4 This crisis demonstrated the dangers of which Cold War policy?

ANSWERS

A1 Cuba requested protection against US attack; short-range missiles on Cuba would balance the US long-range missiles; as a bargaining tool to remove US missiles from Turkey

A2 the presence of the weapons put the USA's major east coast cities in range of nuclear attack

A3 not to invade Cuba; to withdraw US missiles from Turkey

A4 brinkmanship

***examiner's* note** The fact that Kennedy was prepared to stand up to Khrushchev led to greater cooperation between the two men and a slight, albeit temporary, thaw in the Cold War. The 1963 Nuclear Test Ban Treaty followed, as did a direct phone link between the White House and the Kremlin.

69 ANSWERS

Domino theory

Q1 Which US president first introduced the term 'domino theory'?

Q2 This theory led to direct US military involvement in which southeast Asian country?

Q3 What did US involvement in this country initially consist of?

Q4 Which European country also benefited from the domino theory?

ANSWERS

A1 President Dwight Eisenhower

A2 Vietnam

A3 between 1955 and 1959 the USA provided Ngo Dinh Diem, anti-Communist leader of Vietnam, with $3 billion in aid

A4 France; by 1954 it had received $1.4 billion in US aid to help in the struggle against the Vietminh, or Communist guerrillas

examiner's **note** Use your understanding of the domino theory to help explain US foreign policy during the 1960s.

Johnson Doctrine, 1965

Q1 In 1965, Johnson sent 20,000 US troops to which Caribbean country to prevent a socialist government from taking over?

Q2 By increasing the number of US advisers in Vietnam, Johnson continued the policy implemented by which US leader?

Q3 Which incident did Johnson use to argue for the deployment of US combat troops in Vietnam?

Q4 What was 'Rolling Thunder'?

ANSWERS

A1 the Dominican Republic

A2 President John Kennedy

A3 North Vietnamese torpedo boats allegedly attacked US warships in the Gulf of Tonkin in August 1964

A4 a sustained air attack by the USA on key military and industrial targets in North Vietnam; this became the principal weapon used by Johnson to try to force the Communists to the peace table

***examiner's* note** The doctrine reflected Johnson's ardent anti-communism as well as his commitment to global containment starting, specifically, with Cuba and Castro.

Tet Offensive, 1968

Q1 Who were the Vietcong?

Q2 Why were the Americans and South Vietnamese caught off guard by this attack?

Q3 What impact did the offensive have on American public opinion?

Q4 Tet was a decisive event. What did it push President Johnson to announce?

ANSWERS

A1 Communist guerrillas of South Vietnam

A2 it was launched during the Vietnamese New Year, or Tet holiday, when many soldiers were on leave

A3 the American people were deeply shocked; up to 1968 they had been told that the war was being won

A4 that he would not seek re-election as president

examiner's **note** Tet was a major turning point in the war. President Johnson was advised that the war could not be won, even if the 200,000 more soldiers requested by the army were sent to Vietnam. Peace talks began only a few months after the defeat of the offensive.

Tonkin Gulf Resolution, 1964

Q1 The resolution came after which alleged military clash?

Q2 What major power did Johnson gain from the resolution?

Q3 In what way did Johnson escalate the war in 1965?

Q4 What American move followed this escalation?

ANSWERS

A1 the US government maintained that the destroyer *Maddox* had been attacked by North Vietnamese gunboats in international waters

A2 to go to war without first consulting Congress or the American people

A3 by ordering the bombing of North Vietnam on a regular basis

A4 Johnson committed steadily increasing numbers of US combat troops to the conflict

examiner's **note** By passing this resolution, Congress essentially surrendered its powers in the foreign policy decision-making process.

Vietnamisation

Q1 This policy was part of which doctrine?

Q2 Nixon wanted to 'de-Americanise' the war. Why?

Q3 How did the US government plan to continue to support the Saigon government while US troop strength was reduced?

Q4 List the five main points of agreement reached in 1973 by the USA and North Vietnam following peace talks in Paris.

ANSWERS

policy introduced by President Nixon to withdraw US forces from Vietnam

A1 the Nixon Doctrine: the USA would help those nations resisting communism to 'help themselves'

A2 he had campaigned and narrowly won the 1968 presidential election on a promise to withdraw US troops gradually during peace talks

A3 by transferring weapons and equipment to South Vietnamese forces so that Saigon could 'take over' the running of the war

A4 a ceasefire throughout Indo-China; US forces to be withdrawn within 60 days of the ceasefire agreement; the freeing of American POWs; elections to take place in South Vietnam; neither side to launch further offensive operations

***examiner's* note** Vietnamisation caused a split between Nixon and the US military.

Berlin Wall, 1961–89

Q1 Why was Berlin a flashpoint in East–West relations?

Q2 What did the Allies decide should happen with Berlin at the end of the Second World War?

Q3 Approximately how many East Germans left their country through West Berlin between 1952 and 1961?

Q4 Was the Berlin Wall more than simply a wall?

ANSWERS

A1 it was a gap in the Iron Curtain through which East Germans could leave for the West

A2 it was divided into four sectors: Soviet forces occupied the eastern sector while British, US and French forces occupied the western sector

A3 around 3 million; this was about one-sixth of the entire population

A4 yes; armed guards, watchtowers and electric fences discouraged East Germans from attempting to escape

***examiner's* note** The wall was the most powerful symbol of the Cold War. Throughout the Cold War, it was at the heart of the conflict and continued to be a flashpoint between NATO and the Warsaw Pact. The demolition of the wall began in 1989 and Berlin was formally reunited in 1990.

Brezhnev Doctrine

Q1 Of which Soviet leader was this policy the brainchild?

Q2 Which event in 1956 greatly shook Brezhnev and led to his belligerence towards international affairs?

Q3 The Brezhnev Doctrine was employed in 1968 in Czechoslovakia. Explain.

Q4 How did the doctrine reveal a fundamental flaw in the Soviet claim that east European communism was totally unified?

ANSWERS

A1 Leonid Brezhnev, who ruled from 1964 to 1982

A2 the Hungarian Uprising

A3 Brezhnev sent half a million Soviet and Warsaw Pact troops into the country to put an end to a democratic reform movement there

A4 as events in Hungary and Czechoslovakia demonstrated, the USSR was prepared to use force to stop countries in the Warsaw Pact seeking independence from Moscow

***examiner's* note** Western governments scored a major propaganda victory by suggesting that countries behind the Iron Curtain remained Communist only because they were forced to.

De-Stalinisation

Q1 When and where did Khrushchev issue his condemnation of Stalin?

Q2 What was Khrushchev's aim in doing so?

Q3 Khrushchev's idea of 'peaceful co-existence' with the West rested on three principles. What were they?

Q4 The limits of de-Stalinisation were demonstrated by the crushing of pro-democracy movements in which two east European countries?

ANSWERS

A1 during his speech to the 20th Party Congress in 1956

A2 he wanted to bring about greater individual freedom by discrediting Stalin; Khrushchev reduced the power of the secret state police and ordered the dismantling of many state-run labour camps

A3 • war between East and West was not inevitable
   • in the atomic age, Marx's and Lenin's ideas were dangerously outdated
   • the USSR should support communist regimes in other countries through peaceful means

A4 Poland and Hungary

examiner's **note** This policy should not be seen as a sign of greater democratisation in the USSR; Moscow did not allow its satellite states to leave its sphere of influence.

Hungarian Uprising, 1956

Q1 Name the Hungarian Communist leader in 1956.

Q2 Why did the Hungarians revolt against their government?

Q3 What decision by moderate Hungarian leader Imre Nagy resulted in a Soviet invasion of the country?

Q4 Did the Western powers support the Hungarians in their fight for greater freedom?

ANSWERS

A1 Matyas Rakosi

A2 they were encouraged by Soviet leader Khrushchev's suggestion that Moscow would tolerate different types of communism

A3 he announced that Hungary would leave the Warsaw Pact

A4 no; they were preoccupied with the Suez Crisis and unwilling to risk full war with the USSR over the fate of Hungary

examiner's **note** The uprising demonstrated that communism could be maintained in place only by force.

Prague Spring, 1968

Q1 Who was Alexander Dubček?

Q2 Dubček's reforms focused on three main areas of Czech life. What were they?

Q3 What was the major difference between the situation in Hungary in 1956 and that in Czechoslovakia in 1968?

Q4 Why did Soviet and east European leaders order the invasion of Czechoslovakia on 21 August 1968?

ANSWERS

A1 the Czech leader who wanted 'communism with a human face'

A2 • allowing minor parties to join the Communist-run government
• introducing greater democratic rights for the people
• allowing equal rights for the Slovaks

A3 the Hungarian movement was anti-Communist and anti-Soviet,
but Dubček wanted to remain on good terms with Moscow

A4 they feared the Czechs would leave the Warsaw Pact and become
allied with Western countries

examiner's note The invasion of Czechoslovakia brought an end to détente
and marked a deterioration in relations between Moscow and Washington.

Afghanistan: Soviet invasion of 1979

Q1 Why was Afghanistan an unstable country in 1979?

Q2 Afghanistan was strategically important to Moscow. Why?

Q3 Who were the *mujahedeen*?

Q4 List three reasons why Gorbachev ordered a Soviet withdrawal in 1989.

ANSWERS ▶▶

Moscow's strategy to strengthen communism in Afghanistan through military intervention

A1 Muslim opposition groups fought the pro-Soviet government in Kabul, and with some 30 million Muslims in the USSR, Moscow was worried about militant Islam being exported

A2 control of Afghanistan would put the Soviets closer to the middle east and important oil reserves that were so important to the USA

A3 Afghan rebels who waged a 10-year guerrilla war against Soviet forces; they were armed by Pakistan, the USA and China

A4 Soviet involvement was costly, both in human and financial terms; the war was increasingly unpopular and seemingly unwinnable; the Soviet economy was in dire straits and Gorbachev wanted to focus on much-needed domestic reforms

examiner's note It was the last chapter in the Brezhnev Doctrine and marked the end of détente; the USA refused to ratify SALT II, imposed economic sanctions on the USSR and boycotted the 1980 Moscow Olympics.

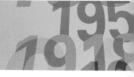

Détente

Q1 Which event demonstrated the danger of military confrontation in the nuclear age?

Q2 List three factors that contributed to a thaw in superpower relations.

Q3 What were SALT I (1972) and SALT II (1979)?

Q4 Why did détente end abruptly and Cold War hostility resume in 1979?

ANSWERS

the easing of tension between the USSR and the USA from 1964 to the mid-1970s

A1 the Cuban Missile Crisis; moreover, by the early 1970s the two sides had the power to destroy each other completely

A2 • both the USA and the USSR faced economic problems
• the USA was looking to end its role in the Vietnam War
• the USSR had begun to fall out with neighbouring China

A3 arms reduction treaties between the two sides that limited the number of missiles and bombers they could have

A4 the USSR invaded Afghanistan to support the country's pro-Soviet government in a civil war; in 1980, the staunchly anti-Communist Ronald Reagan was elected US president

***examiner's* note** The failure of détente led to a new phase of the Cold War and a resumption of the nuclear arms race.

Gorbachev, Mikhail

Q1 In what way was Gorbachev different from his predecessors?

Q2 What were his four main priorities?

Q3 What were superpower relations like during his leadership?

Q4 How did Gorbachev's policies affect the Soviet satellite states?

ANSWERS

leader of the USSR, 1985–91

A1 he concentrated on the USSR's growing internal problems; this led to perestroika (economic reform) and glasnost (liberalising of politics)

A2 • to modernise Soviet industry
   • to ease tension with the USA
   • to halt the arms race
   • to end the Soviet occupation of Afghanistan

A3 they improved significantly; Gorbachev held a series of meetings with President Reagan and they took major steps towards nuclear disarmament

A4 his reforms encouraged the people of eastern Europe to seek change and end communism in their own countries

***examiner's* note** Gorbachev was a driving force behind the end of the Cold War and, ironically, the collapse of the USSR.

Intermediate Nuclear Forces (INF) Treaty, 1987

Q1 What missiles were covered by the treaty?

Q2 Agreement between the two superpowers led to what action?

Q3 Gorbachev made an additional gesture that helped create an atmosphere of trust. What was it?

Q4 Explain the broader significance of the INF Treaty.

ANSWERS ▶▶

A1 medium- and short-range missiles to be used within a continent rather than between continents; many were stationed on UK soil

A2 the destruction of 2,800 missiles, including US Pershing II and cruise missiles, as well as Soviet SS-20 missiles; the presence of these weapons had led to the hardening of détente at the start of the 1980s

A3 he unilaterally reduced his nation's armed forces

A4 it removed a real threat to peace, since the existence of these weapons convinced some on both sides that a limited nuclear war was both possible and winnable

examiner's **note** This was an important step towards establishing good relations between the two leaders and opened the way for the START in 1991.

Reagan, Ronald

Q1 What guided US foreign policy during the Reagan years?

Q2 Three weapons systems developed under Reagan signified the new arms race. What were they?

Q3 Why did the Soviets walk out of the 1985 START talks?

Q4 Which Soviet leader made concessions to Reagan that resulted in nuclear arms reduction treaties between the USA and the USSR?

ANSWERS

A1 his strong anti-communist views; these contributed to an end to détente and a 'New Cold War'

A2 • the neutron bomb
 • Cruise and MX missiles
 • the Strategic Defense Initiative (SDI or 'Star Wars')

A3 they rejected a US proposal for arms reductions in Europe on the basis that it was too one-sided

A4 Mikhail Gorbachev

examiner's note The Reagan presidency witnessed a shift to the right in US politics as well as the collapse of the USSR and the end of the Cold War.

Revolutions of 1989

Q1 List the countries that were involved.

Q2 Why was Romania different to the others?

Q3 Soviet leader Mikhail Gorbachev did three things that many credit with inspiring independence movements in eastern European countries. What were they?

Q4 In 1989 the Soviets responded peacefully to the revolutions. Was this the case previously?

ANSWERS

revolutionary wave that swept across central and
eastern Europe in late 1989 and ended in the rapid
overthrow of Soviet-style communist regimes

A1 Poland, Hungary, East Germany, Czechoslovakia, Bulgaria, Romania

A2 it was the only Eastern-bloc country to overthrow its communist
regime violently; dictator Nicolae Ceausescu was tried and
executed alongside his despised wife

A3 he allowed the Berlin Wall to be torn down, recommended
perestroika in the eastern European satellite states and
renounced the 'Brezhnev Doctrine', which committed Moscow to
using force to protect communist satellite governments

A4 no: Moscow tried unsuccessfully to crush early independence
movements in Lithuania, Latvia and Estonia; this damaged
Gorbachev's credibility and led to the satellite states pursuing
their own independence movements

examiner's **note** The revolutions altered the balance of power dramatically, and
together with the collapse of the Soviet Union in 1991 they ended the Cold War.

Solidarity

Q1 Who was the leader of the Solidarity movement?

Q2 Which group of workers founded Solidarity and why?

Q3 How did the Polish authorities react to Solidarity?

Q4 Why was 1989 a climactic year in Poland?

ANSWERS

Polish independent trade union movement formed in 1980 that resulted in the fall of communism in Poland

A1 Lech Walesa

A2 it began in 1980 as a shipyard workers' protest against high prices and food and fuel shortages in a collapsing Polish economy

A3 in 1982 the military government banned the union and imprisoned its leaders

A4 Poland's leader, General Jaruzelski, arranged free elections in the hope of gaining the support of striking workers; Solidarity won many of the seats in the election and Jaruzelski was forced to appoint a Solidarity member as Polish prime minister — it was the beginning of the end of communism in Poland

examiner's **note** Solidarity became a powerful weapon for President Reagan to undermine the Iron Curtain.

Strategic Arms Limitation Treaties (SALT), 1972 and 1979

Q1 Name the American and Soviet leaders involved with SALT.

Q2 What was the main achievement of the 1972 agreement?

Q3 What type of weapon did the 1979 SALT limit?

Q4 Which event brought SALT talks to a sudden halt?

ANSWERS

A1 Presidents Nixon and Carter (USA) and Brezhnev (USSR)

A2 it limited the building of middle-range weapons for 5 years but did not reduce existing stockpiles of nuclear weapons

A3 long-range nuclear missiles, particularly those with multiple warheads

A4 the Soviet invasion of Afghanistan in 1979, after which the US Congress refused to ratify the agreement

examiner's **note** The failure of the USA and USSR to cap their diplomacy with a concrete agreement resulted in the end of détente and renewed hostility.

Strategic Arms Reduction Treaty (START), 1991

Q1 The treaty was the culmination of negotiations begun in which year?

Q2 Why did the emergence of Gorbachev as Soviet leader in 1985 lead to greater progress in arms reduction talks?

Q3 What stood in the way of a formal treaty before 1991?

Q4 Both Gorbachev and President George H.W. Bush had pragmatic reasons to sign START. What were they?

ANSWERS

agreement signed by the USA and the USSR to destroy about one-third of their nuclear weapons

A1 **1982:** US President Ronald Reagan started talks on how the two sides could not just limit but reduce nuclear weapons

A2 both leaders recognised the financial impact of the arms race and needed to cut costs; this and their constructive working relationship strengthened negotiations

A3 while the two men agreed in principle to an arms reduction, disagreement remained over the US Strategic Defense Initiative

A4 Gorbachev agreed to the treaty in return for much-needed US economic aid; Bush knew the USA was losing its lead in the arms race and did not want to fall behind

examiner's **note** START II (1992) provided for further cuts in each country's arsenal. Both treaties came at the time of the collapse of the USSR and marked the final chapter in the Cold War.

Strategic Defense Initiative (SDI)

Q1 What was the programme's more popular name?

Q2 Explain the main idea behind the project.

Q3 How did the Soviets react to news of SDI?

Q4 Many Europeans did not want to see SDI developed or deployed. Why not?

ANSWERS

US plan for an anti-missile defence system in space

A1 'Star Wars', after the popular 1977 film

A2 the plan was to place a laser shield around the USA to protect it from Soviet intercontinental missiles by knocking them down before they reached their targets

A3 badly: they walked out of the strategic arms reductions talks; the Soviets feared deployment of SDI would upset the balance of power ('Mutually Assured Destruction') by making the USSR vulnerable to long-range missile attack

A4 to some, a protected USA made Europe (where many US missiles were stationed) a more important target for Soviet missiles; Europe could become the battleground for a limited nuclear war

examiner's note The USA invested more than $100 billion in SDI. The system was never fully developed or deployed, but it suggested the US government felt it could wage and win a nuclear war. This led to tension between the superpowers.

Yeltsin, Boris

Q1 Was he was a supporter of Gorbachev?

Q2 Yeltsin was no newcomer to politics in 1991. What led to his rise to national prominence?

Q3 As president, how did Yeltsin attempt to solve Russia's economic problems?

Q4 Yeltsin is remembered for his eccentric behaviour and suspected drunkenness. What caused his ultimate downfall?

ANSWERS

Russian politician, statesman, and president of the Russian Federation 1991–99

A1 no; Yeltsin criticised Gorbachev's reforms as too slow and geared towards propping up a political and economic system he (Yeltsin) opposed

A2 following the August coup against Gorbachev by plotters opposed to perestroika, Yeltsin was credited with rallying mass opposition to the coup by making a highly publicised speech from the turret of a tank outside the parliament building

A3 he embarked on a programme of rapid and radical economic reform geared to converting the world's largest state-controlled economy into a free market economy

A4 his domestic policies were increasingly unpopular; the final straw was his decision to launch the controversial invasion of the breakaway republic of Chechnya in 1994

***examiner's* note** In December 1991, Yeltsin announced the dissolution of the Soviet Union and the establishment of a voluntary Commonwealth of Independent States (CIS). He died in 2007.

Afghanistan: US invasion of 2001

Q1 Who are the Taliban?

Q2 Why did they become the USA's enemy?

Q3 Explain the Taliban threat to neighbouring Pakistan.

Q4 Establishing political stability and national unity in Afghanistan remains elusive. Why?

ANSWERS

military intervention, part of the war on terrorism following the 9/11 attacks

A1 a hardline Islamic group that seized power in Afghanistan following the departure of the Soviets in 1989 and imposed strict *sharia* (religious) law on much of the country from 1994 to 2002

A2 Osama bin Laden resided in Afghanistan before 2001; the Taliban refused to hand him over to the Americans

A3 from the Pashtun tribe, the Taliban are found in areas of northwest Pakistan; they want to rule there and have launched terrorist attacks throughout Pakistan

A4 the terrain, ethnic, religious and regional rivalries, and a state of lawlessness fuelled by the opium trade stand in the way of any central authority

***examiner's* note** Afghanistan's strategic location between the middle east, central Asia and the Indian subcontinent means it has been fought over for centuries. A regrouped Taliban remains a formidable foe.

 ANSWERS

Al-Qaeda

Q1 Who is Osama bin Laden?

Q2 List Al-Qaeda's objectives.

Q3 This organisation has carried out many acts of terrorism. Which remains the most infamous?

Q4 How did the USA respond to this act?

ANSWERS

Arabic word meaning 'the base', used to describe an international Islamist terrorist movement or ideology

A1 a Saudi who is widely regarded as the leader of Al-Qaeda; he first made his name fighting the Soviets in Afghanistan

A2 the end of foreign influence in Muslim countries; destruction of Israel; creation of a global Islamic empire ruled by fundamentalist religious law; jihad (religious war) against Christian countries

A3 on 11 September 2001, terrorists hijacked four US commercial jets: two were flown into the World Trade Towers in New York City, a third hit the Pentagon and a fourth crashed in a rural area; over 3,000 people were killed.

A4 President George W. Bush launched the 'War on Terrorism', beginning with the invasion of Afghanistan (where bin Laden was reportedly hiding) in October 2001

***examiner's* note** Al-Qaeda's killing of innocent civilians – including many Muslims – has seen support for the movement drop around the Muslim world.

Good Friday Agreement

Q1 Who were the main political parties that signed?

Q2 List the main provisions of the agreement.

Q3 Why did the Democratic Unionist Party (DUP) first oppose the agreement?

Q4 Explain the significance of the Good Friday Agreement.

ANSWERS

A1 the British and Irish governments, Sinn Fein, SDLP, Ulster Unionists, as well as some smaller parties

A2 only a majority vote of its citizens could change Northern Ireland's status; all parties agreed to use only peaceful and democratic methods to pursue their goals; establishment of a legislative assembly; power to be shared proportionally; the Irish Republic dropped its claim to the north; decommissioning of paramilitary weapons within 2 years

A3 its leader, Ian Paisley, distrusted Sinn Fein leader Gerry Adams; Paisley later joined the process and served as head of the Northern Ireland government

A4 it ended years of sectarian violence and terrorism, as well as direct rule by London

***examiner's* note** A good knowledge of the main terms of the Good Friday Agreement is essential to understanding its significance.

 93 ANSWERS

Palestine Liberation Organisation (PLO)

Q1 What is the most notable group within the PLO?

Q2 Who was Yasser Arafat and what was his goal?

Q3 How did the PLO pursue its objectives?

Q4 What important event took place in 1993?

ANSWERS

umbrella group for the main armed Palestinian movements with the shared goal of creating an Arab Palestinian state by force and pressure

A1 Al Fatah, a guerrilla organisation set up in the late 1950s

A2 a Palestinian nationalist, guerrilla, statesman and president of the PLO from 1964 until his death in 2004; he wanted the creation of a democratic, non-religious and independent Palestinian state

A3 it waged guerrilla warfare and a campaign of terrorism (bombings, hijackings and the murder of Israeli athletes at the 1972 Olympics) to raise global awareness of Palestinian demands

A4 Arafat rejected the use of terrorism and recognised Israel's right to exist; following direct peace talks, he and Israeli leader Yitzhak Rabin signed an agreement that resulted in Arafat becoming leader of the Palestinian territories on the West Bank and in Gaza

***examiner's* note** The moderation of the Palestine Liberation Organisation led to the rise of more extreme radical Palestinian groups such as Hamas.

Provisional Irish Republican Army (PIRA)

Q1 What is the difference between PIRA and the 'Official IRA'?

Q2 How is PIRA organised?

Q3 List the four prongs of PIRA strategy between 1969 and 1998.

Q4 Who is Gerry Adams?

ANSWERS »

organisation that fought an armed campaign in its struggle for Irish independence from Britain

A1   PIRA is a continuation of the original IRA that fought during the Irish War of Independence; the Official IRA was non-sectarian and believed partition could be ended by a Marxist alliance of Protestant and Catholic working classes

A2   hierarchically; it is led by the seven-man Army Council. Below it are Regional Commands, Brigades and Active Service Units

A3   a war of attrition against security forces in Northern Ireland; a bombing campaign against economic targets; eliminating informers and collaborators; sustaining the war and gaining support at home and overseas through fundraising and propaganda

A4   leader of Sinn Fein, the political wing of PIRA

***examiner's* note** PIRA declared a ceasefire in 1994. Although this broke down temporarily in 1995–97, PIRA did not return to a campaign of violence and decommissioned all its arms in 2005.

Basra

Q1 List the four main British objectives in Basra.

Q2 Why did Moqtada al-Sadr oppose the British presence?

Q3 Who fought in the 2008 'Battle for Basra'?

Q4 British forces handed full control of Basra to the Iraqis on 1 January 2009. How successful was the British mission in Basra?

ANSWERS

port city in southern Iraq, capital of
Basra province and centre of British
operations in Iraq 2003–09

A1 eliminate Baath Party influence; restore infrastructure and services;
provide security; train Iraqi security forces for a handover of power

A2 Al-Sadr is a radical Shia cleric; backed by his militia, known as the
Mehdi Army, he wants Basra governed by fundamentalist *sharia* or
religious law

A3 the Iraqi army, supported by British forces, launched its first
major operation since the 2003 invasion to rid Basra of the anti-
government Mehdi Army

A4 supporters point to security improvements, better opportunities
for women and the weakening of the various militias as successes;
critics maintain corruption is rife and the overall living standard
remains low

***examiner's* note** Britain spent £744 million on reconstruction in and around
Basra. In all, 179 British military personnel were killed during the 6-year presence.

Hussein, Saddam

Q1 Two rival Muslim sects have been responsible for many deaths in Iraq. What are those sects?

Q2 Saddam was an ally of the USA before 1990. Why did his relationship with Washington deteriorate?

Q3 List the factors that caused continued US–Iraq tension after 1991.

Q4 Weapons of mass destruction were central to the US rationale for the 2003 invasion. Did Saddam ever actually use them?

ANSWERS

dictator of Iraq from 1979 to 2003, when he
was overthrown following a US-led invasion

A1 Sunni and Shiite; although very much the minority, the Sunnis held
power over the majority Shiites before 2003 (Saddam was a
Sunni Muslim)

A2 in August 1990, Saddam's forces invaded Kuwait to control its
vast oilfields and gain greater access to the Gulf; in 1991 a US-led
coalition fought a brief but intense war to liberate Kuwait

A3 Saddam's brutal suppression of the Kurds and Shiites; repeated
violations of the UN 'no-fly zone'; Iraq's failure to cooperate fully
with UN weapons inspectors sent to Iraq to find WMD

A4 yes; during the 1980–88 war with Iran he unleashed chemical
weapons on Kurdish civilians, killing thousands

examiner's note Convicted of crimes against humanity, Saddam was hanged
in 2006. In March 2008 the US military officially acknowledged that Saddam had
no direct ties to Al-Qaeda.

 ANSWERS

Iraqi Governing Council (IGC)

Q1 Explain how the IGC was representative of Iraq's diverse religious and ethnic groups.

Q2 List the five main powers the IGC had.

Q3 Did the IGC have legitimacy in the eyes of ordinary Iraqis?

Q4 What was the council's most controversial act?

ANSWERS ▶▶

provisional government of Iraq from July 2003 to June 2004 that was to guide the country until transfer of sovereignty to the interim government

A1 the 25 members included tribal leaders, women, returned exiles, Muslim religious conservatives and secular political leaders; former members of Saddam's Baath Party were excluded

A2 powers to: appoint representatives to the UN; appoint interim ministers to vacant cabinet posts; draft a temporary constitution; propose policies and approve budgets

A3 no; since it was selected and overseen by the US-led Coalition Provisional Authority (which had veto power over the IGC), many Iraqis concluded it was not independent of the occupiers

A4 it replaced the former secular family law code with *sharia* family law, much to the dismay of many Iraqi women who were concerned how it might affect them

***examiner's* note** This diverse group had trouble reaching consensus, but for the first time in Iraqi history the Shiite majority had a leading voice in politics.

'Shock and awe'

Q1 List the four strategic goals of the USA at the start of the Iraq war.

Q2 Why was Iraq's oil production infrastructure an early objective of the invasion?

Q3 On 1 May 2003, President George W. Bush declared the end of major combat operations. This was not the end of the war. Why not?

Q4 What is the human toll of the invasion and insurgency?

ANSWERS

phrase used to describe the opening stage of the 2003 US-led invasion of Iraq

A1 kill Saddam Hussein and his sons; destroy command and control of the Iraqi military; create confusion; destroy the morale of Iraqi forces

A2 prior to the invasion, Iraqi forces had mined some 400 oil wells; the USA wanted to prevent the ecological damage and loss of oil production that followed the 1991 Gulf War

A3 Saddam loyalists, religious radicals, foreign fighters and Iraqis opposed to the occupation launched a deadly insurgency, using tactics including improvised explosive devices (IEDs) and suicide bombers

A4 more than 4,000 US and 179 British service personnel were killed and tens of thousands wounded; estimates of civilian deaths range from 60,000 to 130,000

***examiner's* note** 'Shock and awe' was followed by a swift but intense struggle that saw the collapse of the Iraq government and military in about 3 weeks.

 (99) ANSWERS